SKILL BUILDER GRAMMAR

LEVEL 3

PUFFIN BOOKS

An imprint of Penguin Random House

PUFFIN BOOKS

USA | Canada | UK | Ireland | Australia
New Zealand | India | South Africa | China

Puffin Books is part of the Penguin Random House group of companies
whose addresses can be found at global.penguinrandomhouse.com

Published by Penguin Random House India Pvt. Ltd
7th Floor, Infinity Tower C, DLF Cyber City,
Gurgaon 122 002, Haryana, India

First published in Puffin Books by Penguin Random House India 2021

Text, design and illustrations copyright © Quadrum Solutions Pvt. Ltd 2021
Series copyright © Penguin Random House India 2021

ISBN 9780143445050

Design and layout by Quadrum Solutions Pvt. Ltd
Printed at Aarvee Promotions, India

www.penguin.co.in

Dear Moms and Dads,

There's no better way to prepare your children for their future than to equip them with all the skills they need to grow into confident adults. The Skill Builder series has been created to hone subject skills as well as twenty-first century skills so that children develop not just academic skills but also life skills.

The books in the Skill Builder series focus on numerical, science and English language skills. Recognizing that children learn best while having fun, the books in this series have been created with a high 'fun' quotient. Each subject is dealt with across four levels, so you can choose the level that best suits your child's learning stage.

The Skill Builder: Grammar books have been created by academic experts who have devised a special chart to help you track the skills your child needs to master in order to understand and apply grammatical concepts.

It has been great creating this series with my highly charged Quadrum team—our academic experts, Sutapa Sen and Naimisha Sanghavi, who spent hours crafting each page; Himani, who designed every page to be a visual treat; Gopi, who painstakingly laid out every word; Bishnupriya and Ruby, who read and reread every word; and Kunjli, who was the conscience of the entire series. And of course, the Puffin team—Sohini and Ashwitha—who added value at every step. When you have a great team, you're bound to have a great book.

I do hope you and your child enjoy the series as much as we have enjoyed creating it.

Sonia Mehta
PS: We'd love your feedback, so do write in to us at
funlearningbooks@quadrumltd.com

THE SKILL CHART

Here's a snapshot of the skills your child will acquire as they complete the activities:

- **Reading skills:** The ability to read and comprehend text with proficiency.
- **Writing skills:** The ability to form meaningful sentences and write with proficiency.
- **Speaking skills:** The ability to speak fluently and proficiently in the English language.
- **Punctuation skills:** The ability to use punctuation marks in the correct manner so as to form meaningful sentences.
- **Creative thinking skills:** The ability to view a problem creatively from different angles.
- **Decision-making skills:** The ability to choose between possible solutions to a problem through an intuitive or reasoned process, or both.
- **Critical thinking/problem-solving skills:** Rationalizing, analysing, evaluating and interpreting information to make informed judgements.

Page no.		Reading	Writing	Speaking	Punctuation	Creative thinking	Decision-making	Problem-solving/ Critical thinking
4	KNOW YOUR NOUNS	☺	☺				☺	☺
5	NOUN TRUCK	☺	☺				☺	☺
6	NOUN SORT	☺	☺				☺	☺
7	CONCRETE OR ABSTRACT?	☺	☺	☺			☺	☺
8	INCOMPLETE	☺	☺			☺		☺
9	WHOSE IS IT?	☺	☺		☺		☺	☺
10	REPLACE US	☺	☺		☺		☺	☺
11	ADJECTIVE OR PRONOUN?	☺					☺	☺
12	TRANSITIVE OR INTRANSITIVE?	☺					☺	☺
13	FILL ME CORRECTLY	☺					☺	☺
14	LOOKING FOR OBJECTS	☺				☺	☺	☺
15	HELPING HAND	☺					☺	☺
16	FABULOUS ADJECTIVES		☺			☺	☺	☺
17	SOME OR MANY?			☺	☺	☺	☺	☺
18	DEMONSTRATIVES			☺		☺	☺	☺
19	WHAT'S THE WORD?	☺						☺

KNOW YOUR NOUNS

Identify what type of noun each underlined word is and colour the correct box.

1   I live in a multistorey <u>apartment</u>.

| concrete | abstract |

2   India gained its <u>freedom</u> on 15 August 1947.

| concrete | abstract |

3   Sam's <u>anger</u> makes him unpopular among his friends.

| concrete | abstract |

4   Dona likes to bake <u>cakes</u>.

| concrete | abstract |

5   Soldiers are the <u>pride</u> of a nation.

| concrete | abstract |

6   Shiv and Joe's <u>friendship</u> is an example for eve ryone at school.

| concrete | abstract |

7   Linda rides her <u>bicycle</u> to school.

| concrete | abstract |

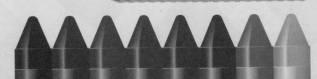

NOUN TRUCK

The truck driver must dump all the concrete nouns.
Write the names of all the concrete nouns you can find
in the spaces provided.

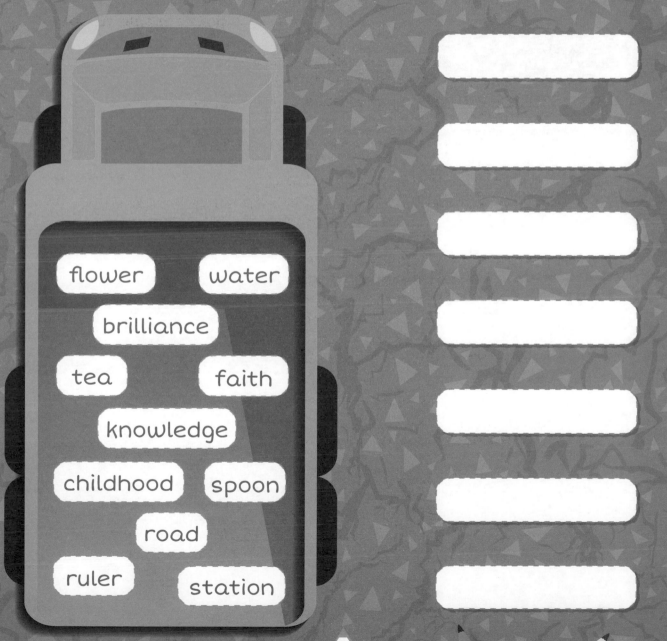

flower   water

brilliance

tea   faith

knowledge

childhood   spoon

road

ruler   station

NOUN SORT

Rewrite the nouns in the box below in the correct columns.

notebook   wisdom   affection   elephant
pride   oven   brother   truth   rainbow
intelligence   perfume   annoyance   table
amazement

Concrete Nouns	Abstract Nouns

CONCRETE OR ABSTRACT?

Make sentences with the nouns given in the box. Then, colour the box that names the type of noun you used.

commitment   street   minerals   sweetness
girl   hatred   belief

1 _____

| concrete | abstract |

2 _____

| concrete | abstract |

3 _____

| concrete | abstract |

4 _____

| concrete | abstract |

5 _____

| concrete | abstract |

6 _____

| concrete | abstract |

7 _____

| concrete | abstract |

INCOMPLETE

Use the possessive pronouns in the box to complete this conversation.

> his   hers   mine   ours   theirs   yours

Nitya: Minnu, I want to go camping this weekend, but we don't have sleeping bags.

Minnu: Why? What happened to your sleeping bags?

Nitya: We have given [_____] to my uncle. Do you think you could lend us [_____] ?

Minnu: But I will need [_____] and my brother has taken the other one with him to his hostel.

Nitya: All right, I will ask Jay if he can give us [_____] and get another one from Sheila.

Minnu: Sheila said she needs to get a new one as [_____] is all worn out.

Nitya: Hmm, then I guess I'll have to ask Karim and his sister for [_____] .

WHOSE IS IT?

Rewrite the following sentences using possessive pronouns. One has been done for you.

This is my book.
The book is mine.

This is your book.

_____

This book belongs
to us.

_____

This is not my book.

_____

REPLACE US

Rewrite the following sentences by replacing the underlined words or phrases with possessive pronouns.

1   <u>Chen's and Ming's</u> drawings won the first prize.

_____

2   <u>Keya's</u> bat is in the car.

_____

3   Have you taken <u>the books that belong to you</u>?

_____

4   Those toys are <u>Rita's and Betty's</u>.

_____

5   The bird was put in <u>the bird's</u> cage.

_____

ADJECTIVE OR PRONOUN?

Circle the words that indicate possession. Then, say whether they are possessive adjectives or possessive pronouns by colouring the right box.

Hint: A possessive adjective is followed by a noun. A possessive pronoun is used alone.

1   That is my study table.

possessive adjective	possessive pronoun

2   The ball is mine.

possessive adjective	possessive pronoun

3   Jina's shoes are black, but yours are white.

possessive adjective	possessive pronoun

4   The students are doing their homework.

possessive adjective	possessive pronoun

5   Your writing is far better than Sam's.

possessive adjective	possessive pronoun

6   That is Tina's racket, but where is yours?

possessive adjective	possessive pronoun

7   His cricket kit has all the required items.

possessive adjective	possessive pronoun

TRANSITIVE OR INTRANSITIVE?

Identify whether the verbs in these sentences are transitive or intransitive by ticking the right box.

Hint: A transitive verb is followed by an object whereas an intransitive verb does not need an object.

		Transitive	Intransitive
1	Please take this letter to Bhim.	☐	☐
2	Johnny played the piano.	☐	☐
3	Nita went to the store to get some tea.	☐	☐
4	I love reading.	☐	☐
5	Ken carried a basket of eggs with him for the guests.	☐	☐
6	It snowed heavily last night.	☐	☐
7	When did you come?	☐	☐

FILL ME CORRECTLY

Fill in the blanks using verbs from the box. You will have to write the verbs in the form that best fits each sentence. One has been done for you.

> collect   rise   go   cost   pay   run   receive

1   The teacher asked the children **to collect** money for the donation drive.

2   The sun _____ in the east.

3   Everyone _____ to the train station together.

4   When can I expect _____ the parcel?

5   By the time I got up, Magnus had already _____ the bill.

6   It _____ fifty rupees to enter the museum.

7   The security guard _____ as fast as he could.

LOOKING FOR OBJECTS

Circle the objects in the following sentences.

1   Andrew gave the hat to Simon.

2   My room gets plenty of sunshine in the mornings.

3   Everybody passed the test.

4   My sick aunt has to take a lot of medicines.

5   Please turn on the television.

6   Ahmad's shoes cost a lot of money.

7   She left the keys on the table.

8   Please get me five books from the library.

HELPING HAND

Circle the main verbs and underline the helping verbs in the following sentences.

1   My sister is playing the piano.

2   They are painting the house.

3   Mr Rao is writing a grammar book.

4   Sarah is skiing on the snow.

5   Doctor Javid has treated my grandmother.

6   Veena is building a sandcastle.

7   Francis can bat for hours.

8   She is driving to the beach.

FABULOUS ADJECTIVES

Choose a descriptive adjective from the box to match each highlighted noun in the sentences below.

> delicious   clever   huge   silver
> beautiful   magnificent   blonde

1   Miranda is a [   ] girl .

2   The roses are [   ] .

3   I loved the [   ] pastries .

4   She was wearing a [   ] ring .

5   The nobleman's horse looks [   ] .

6   Ramona has [   ] hair .

7   The rhinoceros is a [   ] animal.

SOME OR MANY?

Match the sentence fragments to make complete sentences. Then, underline all the quantitative adjectives you see.

I am thirsty. Please could I get	the entire bar of chocolate.
I can lend you a pen. I have	five servings of vegetables every day.
Allen loves sweets. He ate	a little water?
I will finish this book today. There are only	don't like bananas.
I am trying to eat	three pens.
Some people	a few pages left.

DEMONSTRATIVES

Complete the following sentences using demonstrative adjectives—this, that, these, those. One has been done for you.

1. [This] is an umbrella.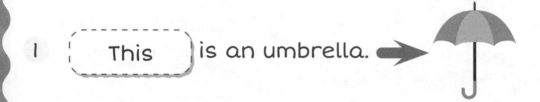

2. [   ] are paper napkins.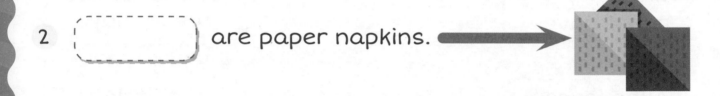

3. [   ] is a dog.

4. [   ] are rabbits.

5. [   ] are mangoes.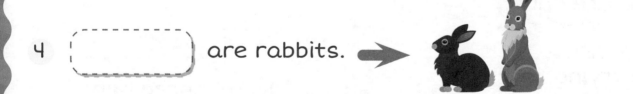

18

WHAT'S THE WORD?

Fill in the blanks with adjectives from the box. Remember to use the correct degree of comparison where necessary!

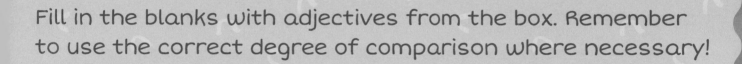

| bad | far | comfortable | good | old | delicious |

1   We had a much [_____] time camping this year than we did last year.

2   Which do you think is the [_____] ice cream flavour?

3   My sister is three years [_____] than me.

4   The buses here are [_____] than the buses in my hometown.

5   Maya lives far from us, but Naina lives even [_____] away.

6   This is a [_____] salad.

19

COMPARISON TIME

Complete this table with adjectives in the correct degree.

Simple	Comparative	Superlative
loud		loudest
	newer	
short		
		coolest
	darker	
slow		
		smallest
	heavier	

Choose two simple adjectives from the table and write a sentence using all three forms of each adjective.

Simple Adjective 1:

Simple Adjective 2:

WHEN DID IT HAPPEN?

Circle the correct option to complete each sentence.

1   We went to the cinema tomorrow/yesterday/next day .

2   Today/now/yesterday is Mother's Day.

3   I will be travelling back home tomorrow/last year/ yesterday .

4   Last year/daily/tomorrow, we celebrated Christmas at my mother's house.

5   I am going to the gym tomorrow/yesterday/now .

6   He received his report card yesterday/now/ tomorrow .

7   It is very cold today/tomorrow/yesterday .

8   Everyone looked for Nina now/yesterday/tomorrow .

22

HOW OFTEN?

Answer these questions about yourself using the adverbs of frequency in the box.

> always   usually   frequently   often
> sometimes   occasionally   seldom   never

1 When do you wake up in the morning?

_____

2 How often do you go to school?

_____

3 How often do you do your homework?

_____

4 When and where do you play outdoors?

_____

5 How often do you visit the library?

_____

6 Do you ever shout at anyone or behave badly?

_____

7 Do you ever try to help people in need?

_____

FUN WITH 'F' AND 'Y'

Complete this paragraph using the correct (singular or plural) forms of the words indicated by the pictures.

School had ended early that day, so Tom, Ravi and Ali went to Tom's house together.

They were hungry. They went to the kitchen and found two _____ (🥖) of bread, some _____ (🍒) and some chocolate _____ (🍰) on the kitchen _____ (▭). Tom's parents weren't at home and the children weren't allowed to use sharp tools without an adult around.

Tom went over to his neighbour's house to ask for help. He found Mrs Spencer with three other _____ (👩). They were busy embroidering _____ (🧵) for a craft fair. Mrs Spencer excused herself and went back with Tom to his house. She found a _____ (🔪) and sliced up a _____ (🥖) of bread and cut some _____ (🍰🍰🍰) of the cake. The three boys enjoyed their snack and thanked Mrs Spencer for her help.

UNUSUAL PLURALS

Write out the nouns pictured here in the first column of boxes. Then, write their plural forms in the second column.

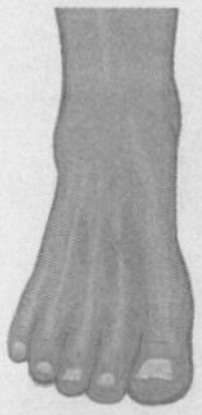

BASKET OF PLURALS

Colour all the nouns whose singular and plural forms remain the same.

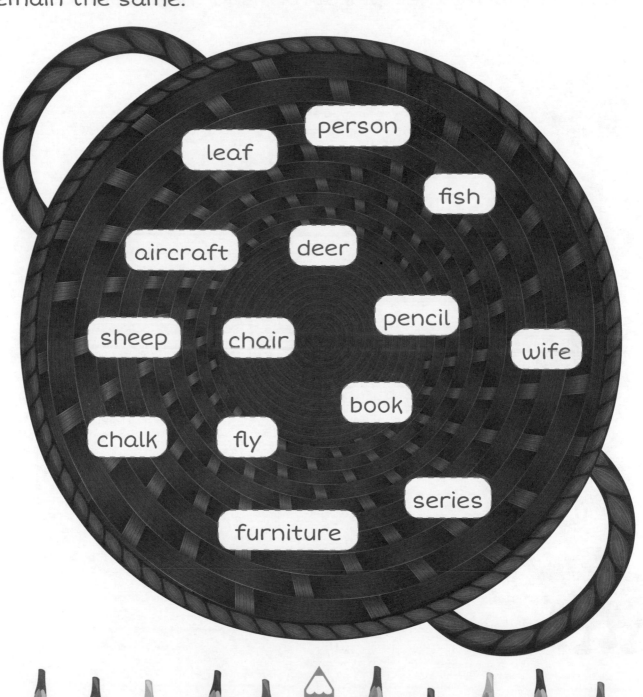

person

leaf

fish

aircraft

deer

pencil

sheep

chair

wife

book

chalk

fly

series

furniture

CONNECT FUN

Choose the correct connecting word to complete each sentence.

1   Octopuses [____] starfish are sea animals.
    but/and

2   I like trekking [____] my brother doesn't enjoy it.
    but/or

3   I have made some chicken curry without green
    chillies specially [____] you. so/for

4   Students may either do a project on history
    [____] geography. and/or

5   He could not tell where he was from the map
    [____] could he see anybody around to ask for
    directions. yet/nor

6   Dona finds arithmetic difficult [____] she tries
    her best to get better at it. or/yet

MORE CONNECTIONS

Use these subordinate conjunctions in sentences of your own.

> because   as   although   after   whether   when

_____

_____

_____

_____

_____

_____

EITHER, NEITHER, WHETHER

Join these sentences with the appropriate correlative conjunctions from the box.

> either/or   neither/nor   not only/but also
> both/and   whether/or   not/but   if/then

1   _____ Linda _____ Aparna are doctors.

2   _____ John _____ Dina was interested in watching the movie.

3   Kunal could not decide _____ to sign up for drama _____ swimming as an after-school activity.

4   You can _____ have an ice cream _____ cold coffee.

5   Ryan is _____ _____ academically brilliant _____ _____ good at sports.

6   It was _____ windy _____ very cold.

STOLEN CONJUNCTIONS

These sentences have been robbed of their conjunctions. Rewrite these sentences using the correct conjunctions and add appropriate punctuation.

> neither/nor   and   but   although
> or   so   not only/but also   when

1   The story is long complicated

_____

2   She does not like to drink tea coffee

_____

3   I lost my wallet. The heel of my shoe broke too

_____

4   Francesca Vidya are dancers

_____

5   He had an umbrella, he got wet in the rain

_____

SEQUENCE CONNECTORS

Fill in the blanks with one of the following sequence connectors.

> first   then   last   later

1   _____ you have to beat the eggs. _____ you pour them into the pan.

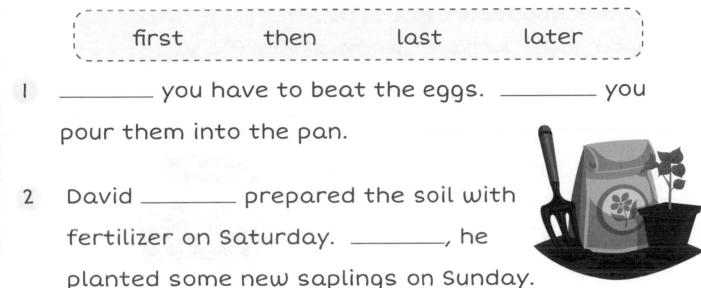

2   David _____ prepared the soil with fertilizer on Saturday. _____, he planted some new saplings on Sunday.

3   Since you are busy now, I'll call you _____.

4   We went to the museum. _____ we got a bite to eat. Our _____ stop before heading home was the grocery store.

5   When he finally got home, his mother cried, 'At _____! I'm so glad you made it.'

OUT OF ORDER

The steps in this cake recipe are all out of order! Write numbers in the boxes to indicate the order in which the steps should appear.

Remember this order: first, then, next, later, finally.

Next, beat the batter until it is smooth.

After that, transfer the batter into a baking pan.

Finally, let it stand for five minutes before you turn the cake out of the pan.

Then, add the vanilla extract, mix again and add milk.

First, mix together the flour, baking powder, butter and sugar.

Later, bake at 250° Celsius for 20 minutes.

CAUSE AND EFFECT

Use **so** to join each sentence in Column A to a sentence in Column B. Then, rewrite the sentences in the space provided.

Column A	Column B
Peter forgot to do his homework.	The students had to wait for the bus.
I did not take a pill.	He had to stay back after school to finish it.
My grandpa fractured his ankle.	The fever did not subside.
School ended early.	He has to walk with the help of a walking stick.

_____

_____

_____

_____

_____

_____

_____

LINKING THEM RIGHT

Use these words and phrases in sentences of your own.

1. because _____

2. as _____

3. since _____

4. therefore _____

5. as a result _____

6. because of this _____

   _____

7. so _____

PAST TIME

Use the past tense form of the highlighted words to complete this paragraph.

It _____ be a cloudy evening. My sister and I _____

finish our homework quickly. Then, we _____ sit

down to watch a cricket match. My mother _____

give us some popcorn as a snack. The match _____ be

an exciting one. However, after an hour, it _____ start

raining. Eventually, the match had to be _____ call

off. My sister and I _____ decide to play a game of

carrom. Then, our mom _____ say it was time for

dinner. After we _____ eat dinner, we _____ go

to bed.

POP CORN

CIRCLE THEM

Circle the past perfect forms of the highlighted verbs to complete these sentences.

1. Max realized that he forgot/had forgotten to pack his English textbook.

2. Sid had not finished/finished the test when the teacher said time was up.

3. She reached/had reached the hospital when I called her.

4. The prize distribution ceremony had started/started, but the chief guest wasn't present.

5. Mike turned/had turned off the air conditioner before the room got too cold.

6. We ate dinner after everybody had returned/returned from work.

7. I had cleaned/cleaned the bathroom, but you have made it dirty again.

PERFECT BUT NEGATIVE

Fill in the blanks with the negative past perfect forms of the verbs in the brackets.

1   We _____ _____ _____ the movie until last night. watch

2   The cook _____ _____ _____ lunch on time. prepare

3   The umpire _____ _____ _____ his finger to declare the batsman out. raise

4   The doctor _____ _____ _____ to discharge the patient. agree

5   The school team _____ _____ _____ a single match in the last two years. win

6   The drought continued because it _____ _____ _____ enough last year. rain

7   I realized that I _____ _____ _____ to my cousin in a very long time. speak

PERFECTLY INTERROGATIVE

Rewrite each sentence in the past perfect tense as a question. One has been done for you.

1   The phone had stopped ringing by the time Neeta got to it.

Had the phone stopped ringing by the time Neeta got to it?

2   Sunny had gone to the market after school.

_____

3   Mr Gupta had sold his land to a builder.

_____

4   Vinay had washed his clothes on Sunday.

_____

5   He had passed the test.

_____

CHOOSE RIGHT!

Choose the correct option to complete the following sentences.

1. Andrew bought three types of biscuits, of _____ I only liked the ones with jam.

   ( ) that   ( ) which   ( ) those   ( ) this

2. Wear the blue scarf _____ has green polka dots.

   ( ) that   ( ) who   ( ) which   ( ) these

3. Show me the lane _____ leads to the park.

   ( ) who   ( ) which   ( ) that   ( ) this

4. _____ of these colours do you like best?

   ( ) whom   ( ) which   ( ) that   ( ) those

5. He will drop off the dress _____ needs to be altered.

   ( ) that   ( ) which   ( ) whose   ( ) whom

WHAT COMES BEFORE?

Write an appropriate prefix in each box below to complete the sentences.

1 I [ ] like going swimming because I am afraid of water.

2 Ryan's test was [ ] complete so he did not do well on it.

3 Your effort this year has been [ ] adequate. You must do better next year.

4 It is [ ] legal to travel without a train ticket.

5 The children were very good and did not [ ] behave at all.

6 I'm so sorry about the [ ] understanding. I'll fix the problem right away.

IN THE END

Add a suffix to each word below to make new words.
One has been done for you.

Words	Suffix	New Word
teach	**-er**	**teacher**
engine		
move		
kind		
fear		
swim		
back		
clock		

PHRASAL VERBS

Fill in the blanks using the correct phrasal verbs from the box. Hint: Keep in mind the tense of the sentence.

throw away	look after	hold on to	run out
break into	turn off	clean up	

1 Shane was _____ _____ before he could score his century.

2 Have you _____ _____ all the broken pencils?

3 You should always _____ _____ the tap after you are done.

4 The vase slipped from my hands and _____ _____ pieces.

5 I _____ _____ my sister when she was ill.

6 Karim _____ _____ the kitchen after lunch was done.

7 Please _____ _____ your hat as it is very windy.

42

SYNONYMOUS

Match the synonyms in the two books below. Circle each pair in a different colour.

One has been done for you.

(quick)   huge

centre

        wonderful

trust

delicious

           prize

gather

           infant

middle

    baby

(fast)

    tasty

belief

amazing

           reward

large

           collect

CREATE AWAY

Add phrasal verbs that contain the words 'get' and 'come' to each web. Then, use any two of them in sentences of your own.

One has been done for you.

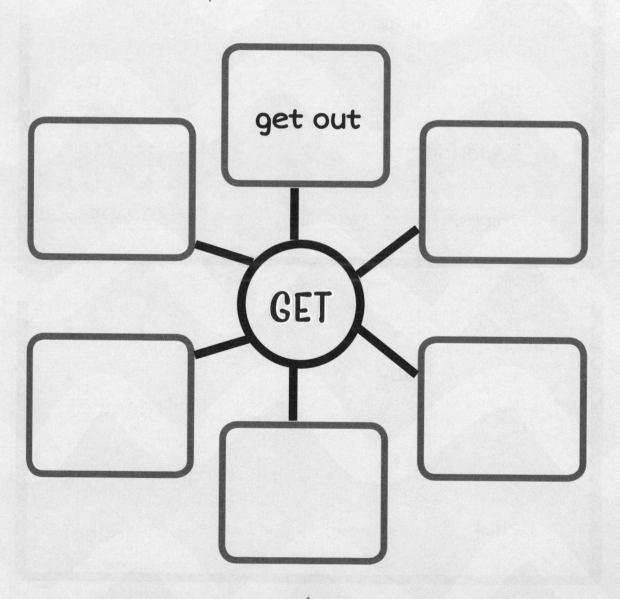

get out

GET

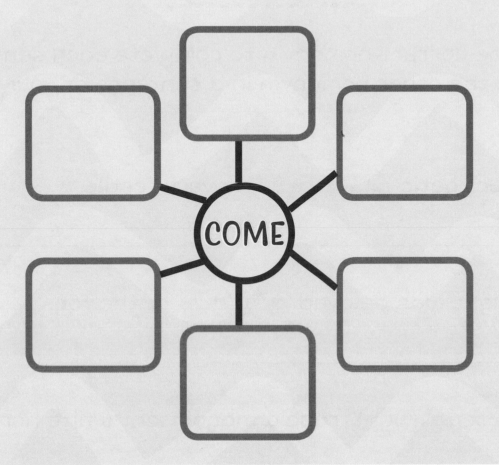

HOMONYMS

Choose the correct homonym to complete each sentence. Then, use the other homonym in a sentence of your own.

1　The Gangetic plane/plain is very fertile.

_____

2　My flight was delayed dew/due to the fog.

_____

3　The night/knight rode a magnificent white horse.

_____

4　Dad asked George to sell/cell his old bicycle.

_____

5　I did not receive any male/mail today.

_____

PUNCTUATE NOW

Rewrite these sentences using punctuation marks and capital letters in the right places.

1   why are you not listening to me

_____

2   hurry up the bus is here

_____

3   your new curtains are very pretty

_____

4   thank you so much for coming i am very happy to
    see you

_____

5   he became very excited and said hooray we have
    won the match

_____

6   look she exclaimed your dress has been spoiled

_____

Use the correct interjections from the box to complete these sentences.

> Hurrah! Oh! Alas! Ouch!
> Hi! Phew! Hey! Wow!

1. _____ My toy train is broken beyond repair.

2. _____ We have won the match.

3. _____ My name is Rina.

4. _____ What a lovely painting!

5. _____ I cut my finger!

6. _____ I didn't know you could play chess.

7. _____ Where do you think you are going?

8. _____ That was a close call!

TAG THEM ALL

Add question tags to these sentences. One has been done for you.

1   Mohan is playing tennis, [isn't it?]

2   They are making clay models, [   ]

3   His brother drives heavy vehicles, [   ]

4   We sometimes watch movies on television,
    [   ]

5   Zuri went to the gym yesterday, [   ]

6   Alannah will arrive today, [   ]

7   This is your pencil box, [   ]

8   You have apologized to him, [   ]

49

STAY POSITIVE

Add positive question tags to these sentences.

1   You aren't coming, [_____] ?

2   You cannot ride a bike, [_____] ?

3   He wasn't hurt, [_____] ?

4   You didn't come to class
last week, [_____] ?

5   He isn't done with his project, [_____] ?

6   You haven't washed the dishes, [_____] ?

7   Veera doesn't practise hard, [_____] ?

8   They couldn't get the tickets, [_____] ?

SUBJECT, PREDICATE

Identify the subjects and the predicates in the sentences below. Then, write them in the correct columns.

1   Madhurima lives in Chicago.
2   Pink and orange are my favourite colours.
3   Hirohito and I were playing chess.
4   My school uniform is crumpled.
5   Dad loves to paint landscapes and portraits.
6   We went to the zoo on the weekend.
7   The horses galloped across the field.
8   Vivek and his sister are always fighting.

Subject	Predicate

WRITE AWAY

Write sentences describing the following pictures.
Circle the subject and underline the predicate.

ASK ME A QUESTION

Rewrite each sentence to turn it into a question.

1   There is a cat in the backyard.

   _____

2   My tennis instructor is coming today at 7.00 p.m.

   _____

3   The sofa needs to be cleaned.

   _____

4   Smita bought an inexpensive dress.

   _____

5   Keshav loves watching football.

   _____

'WH' QUESTIONS

Complete these questions with the right **wh-** words.

1   _____ is the ladder?

2   _____ is the coach of the basketball team?

3   _____ did they leave for the airport?

4   _____ is it important to brush twice a day?

5   _____ is the name of your maths teacher?

WRITE NOW

Write a paragraph about your school. Use as many words from the table as you can. Here are some things you can talk about in your paragraph:

- the name of your school

- how far it is from your home

- how you get to school

- how many friends you have

- your favourite subject and teacher

- what your school looks like

Concrete Nouns	Abstract Nouns	Possessive Pronouns	Descriptive Adjectives	Conjunctions	Sequence Connectors
school					
teacher		ours		and	
classroom	friendship	theirs	beautiful	but	first
friends	intelligence	mine	green	for	later
books	love	his	huge	so	then
blackboard	happiness	her	clever	not	
chalk					

DESCRIBE THE PICTURE

Write a description of this picture in the past tense. Use as many words and phrases from the table as you can.

Subordinate Conjunction	Correlated Conjunction	Adverbs of time and frequency	Phrasal Verbs
because, after, whether	both/and, not only/but also, either/ or	yesterday, all day, sometimes, seldom	ask for, bring along, set up

ANSWERS

page 4 KNOW YOUR NOUNS

1. concrete; 2. abstract; 3. abstract;
4. concrete; 5. abstract; 6. abstract;
7. concrete

page 5 NOUN TRUCK

flower; water; tea; spoon; road; ruler; station

page 6 NOUN SORT

Concrete Nouns	Abstract Nouns
notebook	wisdom
elephant	affection
oven	pride
brother	truth
rainbow	intelligence
perfume	annoyance
table	amazement

page 7 CONCRETE OR ABSTRACT?

Abstract: commitment, sweetness, hatred, belief
Concrete: street, minerals, girl
Sentences will vary.

page 8 INCOMPLETE

ours; yours; mine; his; hers; theirs

page 9 WHOSE IS IT?

This book is yours. OR This book is hers.

This book is ours. OR This book is theirs.

This book is his. OR This book is not mine.

page 10 REPLACE US

1. Their drawings won the first prize. 2. Her bat is in the car.
3. Have you taken your books? 4. These toys are theirs.
5. The bird was put in its cage.

page 11 ADJECTIVE OR PRONOUN?

Words to be circled: 1. my - possessive adjective;
2. mine - possessive pronoun; 3. yours - possessive pronoun;
4. their - possessive adjective; 5. Your - possessive adjective;
6. yours - possessive pronoun; 7. his - possessive adjective

page 12 TRANSITIVE OR INTRANSITIVE?

		Transitive	Intransitive
1	Please take this letter to Bhim.	✔	
2	Johnny played the piano.	✔	
3	Nita went to the store to get some tea.	✔	
4	I love reading.	✔	✔
5	Ken carried a basket of eggs with him for the guests.	✔	
6	It snowed heavily last night.		✔
7	When did you come?		✔

page 13 FILL ME CORRECTLY

2. rises; 3. went; 4. to receive; 5. paid; 6. costs; 7. ran

page 14 LOOKING FOR OBJECTS

1. hat; 2. sunshine; 3. test; 4. medicines;
5. television; 6. money; 7. table; 8. books

page 15 HELPING HAND

Words to be circled: playing, painting, writing, skiing, treated, building, bat, driving;
Words to be underlined: is, are, is, is, has, is, can, is

page 16 FABULOUS ADJECTIVES

1. clever; 2. beautiful; 3. delicious; 4. silver; 5. magnificent;
6. blonde; 7. huge

page 17 SOME OR MANY?

1. little; 2. three; 3. entire; 4. few; 5. five; 6. some

page 18 DEMONSTRATIVES

2. Those; 3. That; 4. These; 5. Those

page 19 WHAT'S THE WORD?

1. better OR worse; 2. best OR worst; 3. older; 4. more comfortable; 5. farther; 6. delicious

pages 20–21 COMPARISON TIME

Simple	Comparative	Superlative
loud	louder	loudest
new	newer	newest
short	shorter	shortest
cool	cooler	coolest
dark	darker	darkest
slow	slower	slowest
small	smaller	smallest
heavy	heavier	heaviest

Sentences will vary.

page 22 WHEN DID IT HAPPEN?

1. yesterday; 2. Today; 3. tomorrow; 4. Last year; 5. now; 6. yesterday; 7. today; 8. yesterday

page 23 HOW OFTEN?

Answers will vary.

page 24 FUN WITH 'F' AND 'Y'

loaves; cherries; cake; shelf; ladies; handkerchiefs OR napkins; knife; loaf; slices

page 25 UNUSUAL PLURALS

mouse, mice; foot, feet; man, men; goose, geese; ox, oxen

page 26 BASKET OF PLURALS

Boxes to be coloured: fish, deer, aircraft, sheep, furniture, series

page 27 CONNECT FUN

1. and; 2. but; 3. for; 4. or; 5. nor; 6. yet

page 28 MORE CONNECTIONS

Answers will vary.

page 29 EITHER, NEITHER, WHETHER

Some possible answers: 1. both/and; 2. neither/nor; 3. whether/or; 4. either/or; 5. not only/but also; 6. not/but

page 30 STOLEN CONJUNCTIONS

1. The story is long and complicated. 2. She neither likes to drink tea nor coffee. 3. Not only did I lose my wallet but I also broke the heel of my shoe. 4. Francesca and Vidya are dancers. 5. He had an umbrella, but he got wet in the rain.

page 31 SEQUENCE CONNECTORS

1. First, then; 2. first, later; 3. later; 4. Then, last; 5. last

page 32 OUT OF ORDER

Next, beat the batter until it is smooth.

After that, transfer the batter into a baking pan.

Finally, let it stand for five minutes before you turn the cake out of the pan.

Then, add the vanilla extract, mix again and add milk.

First, mix together the flour, baking powder, butter and sugar.

Later, bake at 250° Celsius for 20 minutes.

page 33 CAUSE AND EFFECT

1. Peter forgot to do his homework, so he had to stay back after school to finish it. 2. I did not take a pill, so the fever did not subside. 3. My grandpa fractured his ankle, so he has to walk with the help of a walking stick. 4. School ended early, so the students had to wait for the bus.

page 34 LINKING THEM RIGHT

Answers will vary.

page 35 PAST TIME

It was a cloudy evening. My sister and I finished our homework quickly. Then, we sat down to watch a cricket match. My mother gave us some popcorn as a snack. The match was an exciting one. However, after an hour, it started raining. Eventually, the match had to be called off. My sister and I decided to play a game of carrom. Then, our mom said it was time for dinner. After we ate dinner, we went to bed.

page 36 CIRCLE THEM

1. had forgotten; 2. had not finished; 3. had reached; 4. had started; 5. had turned; 6. had returned; 7. had cleaned

page 37 PERFECT BUT NEGATIVE

1. had not watched; 2. had not prepared; 3. had not raised; 4. had not agreed; 5. had not won; 6. had not rained; 7. had not spoken

page 38 PERFECTLY INTERROGATIVE

2. Had Sunny gone to the market after school? 3. Had Mr Gupta sold his land to a builder? 4. Had Vinay washed his clothes on Sunday? 5. Had he passed the test?

page 39 CHOOSE RIGHT!

1. which; 2. that; 3. that; 4. which; 5. that

page 40 WHAT COMES BEFORE?

1. dislike; 2. incomplete; 3. inadequate;
4. illegal; 5. misbehave; 6. misunderstanding

page 41 IN THE END

Words	Suffix	New Word
teach	–er	teacher
engine	–eer	engineer
move	–ment	movement
kind	–ness	kindness
fear	–less	fearless
swim	–ing/–er	swimming/swimmer
back	–ward	backward
clock	–wise	clockwise

page 42 PHRASAL VERBS

1. run out; 2. thrown away; 3. turn off; 4. broke into; 5. looked after; 6. cleaned up; 7. hold on to

page 43 SYNONYMOUS

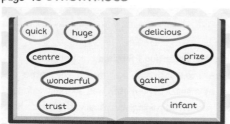

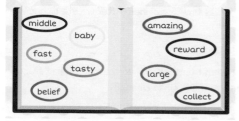

pages 44–45 CREATE AWAY

Answers may vary.

page 46 HOMONYMS

1. plain; 2. due; 3. knight; 4. sell; 5. mail

Sentences will vary.

page 47 PUNCTUATE NOW

1. Why are you not listening to me? 2. Hurry up! The bus is here. 3. Your new curtains are very pretty. 4. Thank you so much for coming! I am very happy to see you. 5. He became very excited and said, 'Hooray! We have won the match!' 6. 'Look!' she exclaimed, 'Your dress has been spoiled!'

page 48 OH MY!

1. Alas! 2. Hurrah! 3. Hi! 4. Wow! 5. Ouch! 6. Oh! 7. Hey! 8. Phew!

page 49 TAG THEM ALL

2. aren't they?; 3. doesn't he?;
4. don't we?; 5. didn't she?; 6. won't she?;
7. isn't it?; 8. haven't you?

page 50 STAY POSITIVE

1. are you?; 2. can you?; 3. was he?; 4. did you?;
5. is he?; 6. have you?; 7. does she?; 8. could they?

page 51 SUBJECT, PREDICATE

	Subject	Predicate
1	Madhurima	lives in Chicago
2	Pink and orange	are my favourite colours
3	Hirohito and I	were playing chess
4	My school uniform	is crumpled
5	Dad	loves to paint landscapes and portraits
6	We	went to the zoo on the weekend
7	The horses	galloped across the field
8	Vivek and his sister	are always fighting

pages 52–53 WRITE AWAY

Answers will vary.

pages 54 ASK ME A QUESTION

1. Is there a cat in the backyard? 2. Is my tennis instructor coming today at 7.00 p.m.? 3. Does the sofa need to be cleaned? 4. How expensive was the dress that Smita bought? 5. What does Keshav love to watch?

page 55 'WH' QUESTIONS

1. Where; 2. Who; 3. When; 4. Why; 5. What

pages 56–57 WRITE NOW

Answers will vary.

pages 58–59 DESCRIBE THE PICTURE

Answers will vary.